# EXTREME!

# Spies

## Amazing Tricks of a Secret Agent

James de Winter

A & C Black • London

Produced for A & C Black by
Monkey Puzzle Media Ltd
Little Manor Farm, Brundish,
Woodbridge, Suffolk IP13 8BL, UK

Published by A & C Black Publishers Limited
36 Soho Square, London W1D 3QY

First published 2009
Copyright © 2009 A & C Black Publishers Limited

ISBN 978-1-4081-1261-8 (hardback)
ISBN 978-1-4081-1990-7 (paperback)

The right of James de Winter to be identified as the
author of this Work has been asserted by him in
accordance with the Copyright, Designs and
Patents Act 1988.

A CIP catalogue record for this book is available
from the British Library.

Editor: Susie Brooks
Design: Mayer Media Ltd
Picture research: Lynda Lines
Series consultants: Jane Turner and James de Winter

This book is produced using paper that is made
from wood grown in managed, sustainable forests.
It is natural, renewable and recyclable. The logging
and manufacturing processes conform to the
environmental regulations of the country of origin.

Printed in Singapore by Tien Wah Press (Pte.) Ltd

Picture acknowledgements
Alamy pp. 13 (Utah Images/NASA), 14 (Photo12),
24 (Photo12); Beijing Military Museum p. 29 top
right; Corbis pp. 4 (Bettmann), 26 (Anna Clopet),
27 (Image Source); Crown Copyright p. 25 all;
Getty Images pp. 1, 5, 9 (Ted Kinsman), 10 left, 15,
17, 21 both (AFP); International Spy Museum pp. 7,
22 left, 29 bottom; Kobal Collection pp. 18 (Cinema
Center), 28 (Danjaq/EON/UA); MPM Images pp.
20, 23 both; PA Photos pp. 8 (Matt Cilley/AP), 19
(David Furst/AP); Photoshot p. 6 (UPPA); Thomas
Jefferson Foundation p. 22 right; Touchstone
Pictures pp. 10–11 (Buena Vista Pictures); US
Department of Defense p. 12; US Navy p. 16.

The front cover shows a spy's eye peeping through
a keyhole (iStockphoto).

Every effort has been made to contact copyright
holders of material reproduced in this book. Any
omissions will be rectified in subsequent printings if
notice is given to the publishers.

# CONTENTS

**Abbreviation  km** stands for kilometres

# Being James Bond

**What's it like to be James Bond? You get gadgets, a cool car, and fame! There are spies like Bond in real life too – but they don't go around being quite so flashy.**

*Klaus Fuchs, a Russian spy, was imprisoned for stealing weapons secrets during World War II.*

K. E. J. Fuchs

## For your eyes only

In the 16th century, a spy working for Queen Elizabeth I marked his secret messages with **00** – a code meaning "for your eyes only". That gave James Bond's creator the idea for 007!

James Bond may be famous, but real spies try hard to stay unknown. Their job is to find out other people's secrets, whether they are war plans, weapons, or just clever ways of making lots of money.

**silencer** a device that absorbs the sound from a gun, making it much quieter

Spy guns can be fitted with **silencers**, so no one will hear the bang.

It might look normal, but this jacket could be bulletproof or contain a hidden camera.

Spying can be dangerous — especially if you're caught. So spies need skill and science on their side. They use the latest technology to help them gather **intelligence** without ending up in prison, or worse.

*James Bond is the spy who will never die — only because he's made up!*

**intelligence** secret information, especially from governments and armies

# Stop bugging me!

**Barging up to the enemy with a film crew would not do a spy any favours. But spies can still record what they shouldn't, using tiny hidden cameras and bugs.**

*This live cockroach is carrying a mini-camera on its back! It can creep under doors to help spies to see what's going on.*

Scientists can now make complicated gadgets smaller than ever before. What looks like a button or a pen lid could be a miniature camera that can take perfect pictures thanks to special lenses inside. A bug the size of an insect can transmit secret conversations to spies listening many miles away. Slip one into a shoe, and you'll always have an ear to the ground...

## Fly on the wall

The US military are working on designs for tiny flying robots that look like insects but have spy cameras and bugs on board.

**bug** a device that records and transmits (sends) sounds to special receivers

The wearer of this shoe becomes a walking radio station.

**2** Recordings are sent out as **radio waves**.

**1** Bug records conversations.

**3** Signal can be picked up many miles away – as long as the batteries don't run out!

Shoe may be worn by a spy or given to the enemy.

**radio waves** waves of energy that travel silently and invisibly through the air

# Eyes in the dark

Under cover of darkness, you can get away with anything – can't you? Think again. Spies have ways of seeing in the dark – and so do their enemies.

## Keeping track

**Thermal imaging** can see where people have been, even if they're not there any more! It can tell where ground has been trodden on, driven on, or dug up to bury something.

*Night vision goggles allow you to see without being seen.*

Our eyes need light to be able to see. But with night vision equipment, a spy can snoop for secrets in a pitch-black room. Some **night vision** gadgets collect up tiny amounts of light that we don't notice. Others use thermal imaging to detect warm things like people... including spies escaping on the run.

**thermal imaging** making pictures using infrared heat energy instead of light

_A thermal imaging camera catches people walking in the woods._

People give off heat, even when standing still.

Don't run – you'll just get hotter, brighter and easier to spot!

Trees and ground show up a different colour because they are cool.

**night vision**  ability to see in the dark using infrared heat energy

# I see-see TV you!

A safe way of spying is to do the job from a distance. With **CCTV**, spies can stay hidden — and have eyes in hundreds of places at once.

> Many different cameras can be watched at once.

*This CCTV picture helped to identify four terrorists who bombed a London bus and underground trains in July 2005.*

*CCTV cameras send their pictures by wires or radio waves to screens in control rooms like this.*

**CCTV (closed-circuit TV)** a way of filming streets, shops and other places

CCTV cameras lurk in all sorts of places, filming all day every day. They may spot a suspect wandering home, or catch a criminal in action. The pictures are transmitted to nearby TV screens, and saved onto giant computers. This helps spies, police and governments to track down trouble, without having to budge from their seats.

## Always watching

There are millions of CCTV cameras in the UK. Some of us may be filmed over 300 times a day. Make sure you behave yourself!

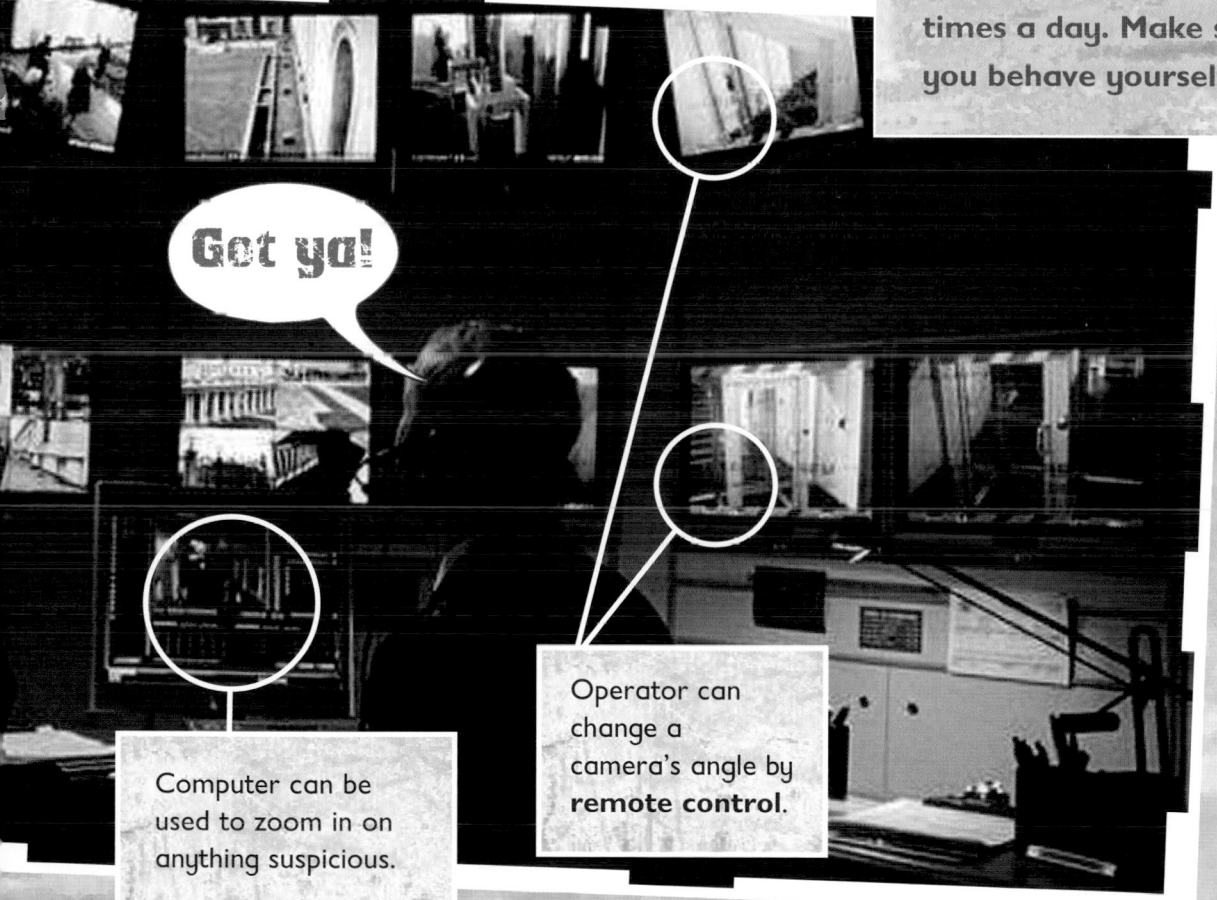

Got ya!

Computer can be used to zoom in on anything suspicious.

Operator can change a camera's angle by **remote control**.

**remote control** operating a device from a distance, often using radio signals

# High spy!

Imagine terrorists were planning to attack your country. How would you find their base? You'd get a pretty good view from the sky – and an even better one from space.

Satellite photos can show up a vehicle, but not quite its number plate.

*A satellite photograph reveals a terrorist training camp in Afghanistan.*

Spy **satellites** act like massive digital cameras, travelling around the Earth in space. They take pictures of the ground below them as they pass over, using gigantic lenses to zoom close-in. Information about how they work is mostly top secret, but we know that they beam radio signals back to Earth. These are captured by spy computers, which display the photos on screen.

## Flying photos

Early spy satellites delivered their pictures by dropping camera film attached to parachutes. Military planes would catch them in mid-air!

**satellite** a machine that is sent into space to collect and send back information

Satellites fly 160–2,000 km (100–1,240 miles) above the Earth.

*A spy satellite orbits the Earth.*

Gravity and high speed keep the satellite moving in a circular path.

Radio signals beam pictures back to Earth.

**gravity** a pulling force between all objects in the universe

13

# Snooperscopes

**You're under the sea in a secret submarine, spying on enemy ships. No one can see you deep down there – but you can see them, thanks to a periscope.**

*Sean Connery looks into a submarine periscope in the film The Hunt for Red October.*

Periscopes allow spies to see round corners, over walls – and up through the ocean. They work by using mirrors or **prisms** to bounce light from one place to another. A mirror at the top of the periscope **reflects** light down into a second mirror at the bottom. This then reflects the light towards the viewer's eye.

The most advanced periscopes have lenses in the middle of the tube. These enlarge the view you see, so the periscope acts as a telescope too!

## Sneaky specs

Have you ever wished you had eyes in the back of your head? Some spies wear sunglasses with mirrors on the inside, so they can see what's going on behind them!

**prism** a triangular block of glass or plastic that can bend the path of light

Mirror inside the tube reflects light down to the bottom.

Mirrors must be set at exactly the right angle.

You're being watched if you're over here!

Light travels down through the periscope.

Light reflected in bottom mirror is sent towards the eye.

*A Kosovan soldier keeps an eye on the enemy using a home-made periscope.*

**reflect** to bounce back rays of light

15

# Invisible ears

**Spies might check their rooms for bugs and make their phone calls in private – but that doesn't mean no one hears what they say.**

*Inside this **radome**, anyone's mobile phone conversation could be recorded – even yours.*

Every phone call, fax and e-mail that's ever sent is transmitted along wires or as radio waves though the air. **Intelligence networks** have special equipment that can intercept these messages and find out what anyone is saying. If spies want to know what foreign spies are up to, they can search for certain keywords. Computers will pick these words out of all the waffle, saving a lot of listening time!

**radome** a weatherproof dome covering radio receivers

Hidden receivers capture radio, phone, fax and e-mail conversations.

On-board computers work out which messages matter.

Jibber jabber

# Global ears

**ECHELON** is a secret spy system that governments use to tap into communications around the world. It recognizes words in every single language!

*This US spy plane is like a vacuum cleaner in the sky, sucking up everyone's words!*

**intelligence networks** groups of spies working for governments or businesses

# Masters of disguise

If you ever met a spy, you probably wouldn't know it. In fact, the American woman you're talking to might actually be a Russian man! Spies need to blend in with whoever they're watching – which is why they are masters of disguise.

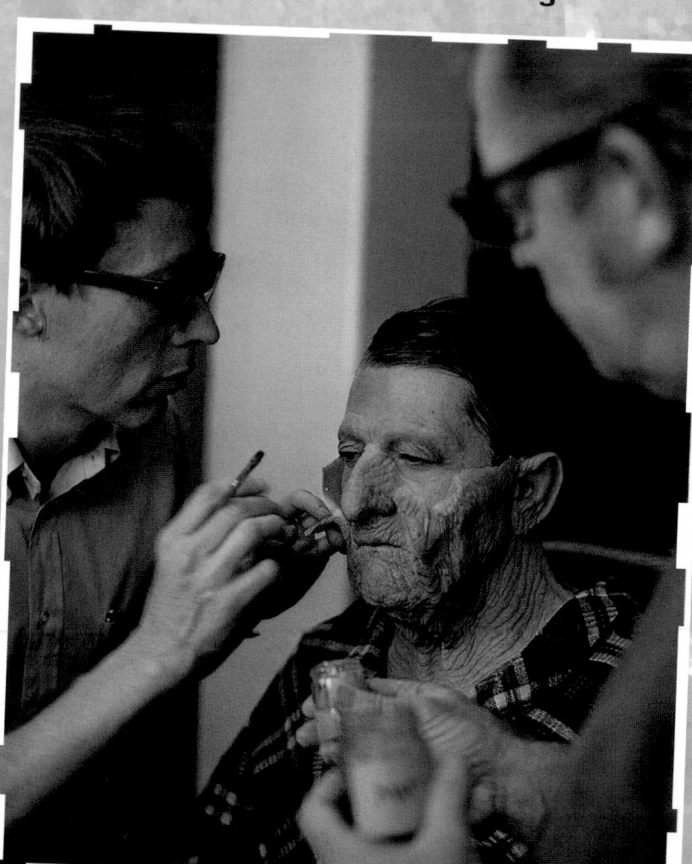

Today's spies have impressive wigs, make-up and even **voice changers** to help them create a **cover**. They may spend years and years pretending to be someone else – but, these days, that's not as easy as it sounds.

Computers can now recognize your walk, sniffer dogs can tell your smell... and even if you manage to change these things, your eyeballs will give you away.

*With modern make-up, you really can get into someone else's skin! Is he who he says he is?*

**voice changer** a device that changes the sound of your voice

18

*A man has his iris scanned at a security check.*

Machine scans the eyeball.

Everyone's iris is unique.

Details about the person are kept on file.

Scanner works even through contact lenses.

## Eye spy

The coloured part of your eye, called the iris, has a pattern unlike anyone else's. Just like fingerprints, it can be scanned and used to prove who you are!

**cover** a false identity

19

# Dead-letter box

**A dead-letter box sounds like something used by a corpse – but in fact it's a place where spies leave secret messages! Spies do this when it's too dangerous for them to meet.**

Messages need to be hidden where they won't **rot**, blow away or get eaten by a curious animal. One trick is to bury them underground inside sealed metal spikes, which won't let in air or water. A chalk cross on a wall or chewing gum on a lamp post can show that a message has been left. Nowadays, spies use **electronic** messages, as well as written ones.

*Secret messages, money or maps might be rolled up and buried in these **dead drop** spikes.*

## Message not sent

**Some terrorists share e-mail accounts, writing draft messages to each other but never sending them. Governments can't scan unsent e-mails, so they aren't spotted.**

**rot** to break down or decay   **electronic** using or controlled by computers

In 2006, the Russian government said they'd caught British spies who had been using a message transmitter disguised as a rock.

EuroNews

07:38 New York
13:38 Bruxelles
15:38 Moscow

Spy's face is covered up to hide his identity.

Upside-down in the snow, you won't see this give-away lid.

Inside, a secret transmitter communicates with nearby computers.

What's this? A rock?

**dead drop** (or dead-letter box) a place where hidden messages are left

# Gobbledegook?

**Spies need to tell each other things without any of their enemies understanding. That's why they make up brain-boggling, gobbledegook codes.**

The science of code making and breaking is called cryptography. When codes were first invented, they had to be cracked by brainy people using pens and paper! Then special machines were invented to do the job. These days spies use **supercomputers** to turn words, numbers and even pictures into code — and translate them back again.

This code-making, code-breaking machine called Enigma was invented at the end of World War I.

The third US president, Thomas Jefferson invented this **cipher** wheel.

Dots on the wings stand for guns.

Lines lead into the fort, showing where the guns are positioned.

*Some spies hid secret maps in drawings. Inside this picture of a butterfly is a map of a fort and its guns.*

Outline of fort

# A heavy read

**The British Navy used to write codes in books with heavy lead covers. If a ship was captured, the crew could throw the books overboard and they'd quickly sink.**

*Moving the wing dots inwards showed where the guns were kept.*

**cipher** a way of replacing each letter in a message with another letter to hide its meaning

# Disappearing words

No matter how good your eyesight, some secret messages are impossible to see. Spies aren't magicians — but they can make their writing disappear!

A **microdot** camera can take a picture so small, it would fit this whole page into a full stop! During World War II, spies sneaked many secret plans past the enemy in this way.

A microdot message was impossible to read — unless you had a microscope. Lenses in the microscope made the dot look hundreds of times bigger, and so the writing became clear.

*Lemon juice is used as invisible ink in the film National Treasure. Onion juice, milk and soapy water work too!*

## Invisible ink

If you write a message in lemon juice, no one can see it. But heat it up on a radiator and the words will magically reappear! Spies use chemical **reactions** like this to create all sorts of invisible inks.

**microdot** a tiny dot that contains secret information

**1** At first glance, this looks like an ordinary watch.

**2** Look closer and you can see a tiny smudgy mark at the bottom of the watch face.

*More than just a gift from one spy to another – this watch carried top-secret information.*

**3** Under a microscope, all becomes clear – it's a secret message.

**reaction** a chemical change caused by heating or mixing chemicals

# Truth and lies

What does a spy dread most? Getting caught! It's hard to hide what you're up to when spycatchers have machines that can tell if you're fibbing.

**Are you a spy?**

**No, I'm not!**

*Is she telling the truth? A lie detector (or polygraph) will reveal the answer.*

Even if you're a brilliant actor, tiny changes in your body can give you away as an **impostor**. When you're nervous your heart pumps faster — and this can happen when you're lying too. Lie detectors measure your **heart rate** as well as how much you sweat, how quickly you are breathing and other things that show you might be hiding something.

**impostor** someone pretending to be someone else

*A voice-recognition system can help to detect an impostor.*

Shape of your mouth and throat affects your voice.

VOICE MATCH - R WAV

NAME : M.REDCLIFF
ID : J669549J-1
ACCESS : GRANTED

EXTERNAL MICROPHONE

RATE = 008 BPS
PITCH = 0.61

PEAK DB 2/110

WAVE / 17

001011001110

Computer recognizes tiny differences between one voice and another.

Even voices that sound the same to a human ear look different on the computer screen.

# Brain wave

People can train their bodies to cheat lie detectors. But new types of machine that scan the brain may be able to catch out even the cleverest spies.

**heart rate**  the number of times your heart beats in one minute

# Kiss of death

Spies love secret weapons, from poisoned knitting needles to lipsticks with guns inside. Throughout the years there have been more deadly gadgets than in a James Bond film.

*An accident waiting to happen? This exploding plaster cast was used in the Bond film Goldeneye.*

## No smoking!

Stories say that in the 1960s, US spies planned to kill Cuban leader Fidel Castro – using an exploding cigar! The plot probably didn't really exist, though.

Some famous hidden weapons include a pipe with a pistol inside, a chocolate bar bomb and an umbrella with a poisoned spike. The more ordinary the object, the bigger the deadly surprise!

In the past, a good hiding place and a bit of imagination allowed spies to get away with murder. But today's **metal detectors**, **X-ray** machines and sniffer dogs can find even the best secret weapons.

**metal detectors** devices that use magnets to find hidden metal

*Shake this hand and you'll never forget it.*

Cap hides true purpose of the "lipstick".

Gun is hidden in the glove palm.

Twist here to fire.

The Russian secret service, the KGB, gave this lipstick gun to female agents to kiss the enemy goodbye.

Barrel of gun

Single bullet means you only get one shot.

**X-rays** invisible waves of energy that can be used to see through objects

# Glossary

**bug** a device that records and transmits (sends) sounds to special receivers

**CCTV (closed-circuit TV)** a way of filming streets, shops and other places

**cipher** a way of replacing each letter in a message with another letter to hide its meaning

**cover** a false identity

**dead drop** (or dead-letter box) a place where hidden messages are left

**electronic** using or controlled by computers

**gravity** a pulling force between all objects in the universe

**heart rate** the number of times your heart beats in one minute

**impostor** someone pretending to be someone else

**intelligence** secret information, especially from governments and armies

**intelligence networks** groups of spies working for governments or businesses

**metal detectors** devices that use magnets to find hidden metal

**microdot** a tiny dot that contains secret information

**night vision** ability to see in the dark using infrared heat energy

**prism** a triangular block of glass or plastic that can bend the path of light

**radio waves** waves of energy that travel silently and invisibly through the air

**radome** a weatherproof dome covering radio receivers

**reaction** a chemical change caused by heating or mixing chemicals

**reflect** to bounce back rays of light

**remote control** operating a device from a distance, often using radio signals

**rot** to break down or decay

**satellite** a machine that is sent into space to collect and send back information

**silencer** a device that absorbs the sound from a gun, making it much quieter

**supercomputers** very advanced computers that work extremely quickly

**thermal imaging** making pictures using infrared heat energy instead of light

**voice changer** a device that changes the sound of your voice

**X-rays** invisible waves of energy that can be used to see through objects

# Further information

## Books

***Secrets, Lies, Gizmos and Spies: A History of Spies and Espionage*** by Janet Wyman Coleman (Harry N. Abrams, Inc, 2006)
A full history of spying through the ages with lots of excellent photographs from the International Spy Museum in the USA.

***Spies*** by Clive Gifford (Kingfisher Books, 2007)
Plenty of information on codes, disguises and famous spies through the ages.

***Stormbreaker*** by Anthony Horowitz (Walker Books Ltd, 2005)
A gripping novel about 14-year-old Alex Rider who discovers secrets about his uncle and becomes a spy.

## Websites

**www.fbi.gov/fbikids.htm**
The children's section of the official FBI website has games, stories and interactive activities arranged by age group.

**www.simonsingh.net/ The_CDROM.html**
Download a free CD-ROM with lots of secret codes and code-breaking activities and information.

**www.spymuseum.org**
This US museum is dedicated to spying, with downloadable activities in the games section and teacher guides in the educator section.

**www.sciencemuseum. org.uk**
Type "spies" or "spying" into the search box to find activities and information from the London Science Museum.

## Films

***Spy Kids*** directed by Robert Rodriguez (Miramax Films, 2001)
A funny and exciting film about a brother and sister who have to help their spy parents out on missions. Features lots of cool gadgets.

***Stormbreaker*** directed by Geoffrey Sax (Entertainment Film Distributors, 2006)
Almost as great as the book; Alex Rider is a teenager who joins the British secret services. Fun for adults and children with an all-star cast.

***National Treasure*** directed by Jon Turteltaub (Buena Vista Pictures, 2004)
A treasure hunter uses codes and other spy techniques to track down lost treasure.

# Index